T0413368

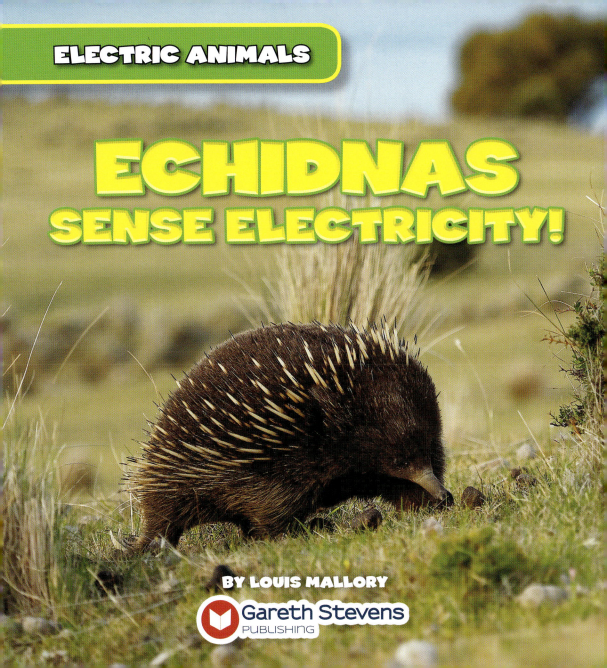

ECHIDNAS SENSE ELECTRICITY!

BY LOUIS MALLORY

Gareth Stevens
PUBLISHING

Please visit our website, www.garethstevens.com. For a free color catalog of all our high-quality books, call toll free 1-800-542-2595 or fax 1-877-542-2596.

Cataloging-in-Publication Data
Names: Mallory, Louis.
Title: Echidnas sense electricity! / Louis Mallory.
Description: New York : Gareth Stevens Publishing, 2024. | Series: Electric animals | Includes glossary and index.
Identifiers: ISBN 9781538292877 (pbk.) | ISBN 9781538292884 (library bound) | ISBN 9781538292891 (ebook)
Subjects: LCSH: Tachyglossidae–Juvenile literature.
Classification: LCC QL737.M73 M355 2024 | DDC 599.2'9–dc23

Published in 2024 by
Gareth Stevens Publishing
2544 Clinton Street
Buffalo, NY 14224

Designer: Claire Wrazin
Editor: Natalie Humphrey

Photo credits: Cover, p. 1 Martin Pelanek/Shutterstock.com; background (series art) Romashka2/Shutterstock.com; p. 5 Kima/Shutterstock.com; p. 7 Janelle Lugge/ Shutterstock.com; p. 9 (platypus) worldswildlifewonders/Shutterstock.com, (echidnas) Paul Looyen/Shutterstock.com; p. 11 Heatherfaye/iStock; p. 13 Ken Griffiths/Shutterstock.com; p. 15 mxk_russ/Shutterstock.com; p. 17 LKR Photography/Shutterstock.com; p. 19 Witsawat.S/Shutterstock.com; p. 21 Patrick Tangye/Shutterstock.com.

Printed in the United States of America

CPSIA compliance information: Batch #CW24GS: For further information contact Gareth Stevens, New York, New York at 1-800-542-2595.

Find us on

CONTENTS

Boldface words appear in the glossary.

Sensing Electricity

Echidnas are special animals that you can find in the wild only in Australia and New Guinea. But that's not the only interesting fact about them. Echidnas have an extra sense that helps them find food. They use their **sensitive** noses to sense **electricity**!

An Echidna's Body

An echidna is 14 to 30 inches (36 to 76 cm) long and weighs 6 to 22 pounds (3 to 10 kg). Echidnas are also called spiny anteaters. This is because echidnas are covered in **spikes**, or spines, that keep them safe from predators.

Monotremes

Echidnas are part of a group of animals called monotremes. Monotremes are the only **mammals** that lay eggs. Monotremes are also the only known mammals that can sense electricity. Platypuses are also part of this family.

PLATYPUS

Receptors

An echidna's nose is called a beak. An echidna's beak has special **receptors** that sense electricity. Echidnas usually have around 400 receptors in their beak. Some echidnas have up to 2,000 receptors!

The receptors in an echidna's beak can **detect** bugs moving in the ground. When the bugs move, their bodies make a small amount of electricity. The echidna senses this electricity, and it uses its large claws to dig the bugs out.

Long Tongues

After the echidna digs out the bugs, it uses its long **tongue** to lick them up. Echidna tongues are very thin and sticky, and are more than 6 inches (15 cm) long. That's about twice the length of a human tongue!

Bug Paste

Echidnas don't have teeth. This means they can't chew their food. Instead, after an echidna licks up its meal, it squashes the food against the roof of its mouth. This makes a bug paste the echidna can swallow.

Tasty Termites

Echidnas eat many kinds of bugs, but there is one they like more than others! **Termites** are their favorite meal. This is because termites are not as hard to eat as other bugs. If there aren't any termites nearby, an echidna will also eat ants, beetles, and worms.

TERMITE

19

Other Senses

Scientists aren't sure how often echidnas use their talent of sensing electricity. They have other receptors that help them sense touch, sound, and movement. They use these and a strong sense of smell to help them find food too.

GLOSSARY

detect: To notice or discover the existence of something.

electricity: A kind of energy that flows and is made by the movements of animals.

mammal: A warm-blooded animal that has a backbone and hair, breathes air, and feeds milk to its young.

receptor: Part of an animal's body that senses changes in its surroundings, like hot or cold.

sensitive: Able to sense or feel changes in surroundings.

spike: A long, thin rod that ends in a point.

termite: A small insect that eats wood.

tongue: The soft part inside of an animal's mouth usually used for tasting food.

FOR MORE INFORMATION

BOOKS

Anlauf, Lena, and Vitali Konstantinov. *Genius Noses: A Curious Animal Compendium.* New York, NY: NorthSouth, 2023.

Lesley, John. *Echidna.* Sydney, Australia: Redback Publishing, 2023.

WEBSITES

Active Wild: Echidna Facts
www.activewild.com/echidna-facts/
Watch videos and learn more fun facts about echidnas.

San Diego Zoo Wildlife Explorers: Echidna
www.sdzwildlifeexplorers.org/animals/echidna
Learn more about how echidnas live in the wild.

Publisher's note to educators and parents: Our editors have carefully reviewed these websites to ensure that they are suitable for students. Many websites change frequently, however, and we cannot guarantee that a site's future contents will continue to meet our high standards of quality and educational value. Be advised that students should be closely supervised whenever they access the internet.

23

INDEX